Living with Trust in the Higher Power

Margot Sinclair

The Cosmic Comedy

In a world swirling with uncertainty, chaos, and doubt, you might be tempted to think that we're all just cosmic debris, drifting through a universe indifferent to our plight. After all, if you squint hard enough at the night sky, the stars look like pinpricks of light in a vast, black abyss—each one a reminder of just how insignificant we are. Or so it seems.

But what if I told you that's all a grand, cosmic joke? That behind the veil of existential dread, there's an unseen hand, a higher power—call it the Great Cosmic Organizer—guiding us, protecting us, even when we can't see the puppet strings? Think of it as the universe's way of giving us a pat on the back while we're busy stumbling through life's absurdity.

You see, the universe has a peculiar sense of humor. It's like a cosmic comedian playing an elaborate prank on us. Picture this: every misstep, every heartbreak, every fleeting moment of despair, is merely the setup for the punchline we're yet to understand. We might be lost in the dark, but there's a guiding light—faint, perhaps, but persistent. This higher power, or however you want to label it, is the unspoken architect of our existence.

So, let's embark on this journey together. We'll dive into the grand, quirky scheme of things, exploring how this unseen force weaves through our lives like a cosmic weaver. Amidst the mess and the muddle, there's a pattern, a design—one that's far grander and more absurdly beautiful than we could ever imagine. Welcome to the great cosmic comedy, where even in the chaos, there's an underlying order, and perhaps, just perhaps, we're not as alone as we sometimes feel.

This introduction aims to set a tone that combines Vonnegut's characteristic mix of dark humor and existential reflection, while gently introducing the concept of a higher power.

The Infinite Embrace

When we speak of the omnipotence of the higher power, we're talking about a force so boundless that no corner of existence is beyond its reach. Imagine, if you will, a maestro orchestrating the grand symphony of the cosmos—a conductor whose baton directs not only the crescendos and diminuendos of celestial bodies but also the quiet whispers of the breeze as it rustles through the leaves.

This higher power, this cosmic force, is not a distant deity watching from afar, but the very essence that permeates every atom of our being. It is the silent architect of every moment, from the growth of a seed breaking through the soil to the colossal collapse of a dying star. Every detail, from the grandest of events to the humblest of occurrences, is woven into the fabric of its will. Even in the midst of chaos, when life seems a jumbled mess of fragmented experiences, this power is the unseen hand that keeps it all in place. It is the unifying thread in the tapestry of existence, the alpha and the omega of every universe—seen and unseen.

To say that everything is part of this higher power is not merely a poetic metaphor but a profound truth. We are not separate entities drifting through a void; we are integral parts of a magnificent whole. The chair you're sitting on, the sky stretching endlessly above you, the flood of emotions that sweep through you—all of these are infused with the essence of this higher force. It's a living, breathing reality that transcends abstract concepts, manifesting in every experience and every breath you take.

When we recognize that everything is Him, we acknowledge that the higher power is not confined to sacred texts or holy places but is embedded in the very fabric of our daily lives. It is in the mundane and the monumental, the joyous and the sorrowful. It is the omnipresent energy that guides us through the labyrinth of existence, reminding us that even in our most solitary moments, we are never truly alone.

So, as you navigate the winding paths of your own journey, remember that you are always held in this infinite embrace. The higher power is not a distant observer but a constant companion, shaping every experience and every moment with its boundless grace.

In recognizing this, you may find solace and strength, knowing that you are never beyond the reach of this eternal force.

The Symphony of Significance

When we come to recognize the omnipresence of this higher power, our perception of life transforms profoundly. We shift from seeing ourselves as solitary wanderers in a vast, indifferent universe to becoming participants in a grand, orchestrated symphony. Suddenly, the notion that we are alone, navigating a world that sometimes seems capricious and devoid of meaning, gives way to a deeper understanding that every moment, every experience, is imbued with significance.

Imagine life as an intricate tapestry woven by a divine hand, where each thread, no matter how seemingly insignificant, contributes to the overall design. From the fleeting joy of a shared smile to the heart-wrenching sorrow of a loss, every experience is a stitch in this grand fabric. We might not always grasp the pattern or understand the purpose behind each moment, but that doesn't diminish its value or impact.

This realization—that there is a higher power orchestrating the seemingly random events of our lives—offers a profound comfort. It's akin to discovering that behind the chaos of a storm, there's a masterful hand guiding the winds and rain, shaping them into a necessary part of the greater design. Even when life seems arbitrary and disconnected, the knowledge that there is divine intelligence at work can instill a sense of peace and reassurance.

Every moment carries meaning, whether we can decipher it or not. Each experience, every joy, every challenge, serves a purpose in the grand scheme of things. The higher power's control over all things assures us that nothing is ever truly random or meaningless. Even in our darkest times, when the path ahead seems shrouded in uncertainty, we can find solace in the understanding that there is a greater plan unfolding, one that is beyond our immediate comprehension but ultimately for our growth and well-being.

Embracing this reality—that the higher power is the guiding force behind all things—allows us to see life through a lens of deeper meaning and purpose. We are not mere spectators of our own lives but active participants in a divine play where every act, every scene, contributes to the unfolding story. With this perspective, we can navigate the ups and downs with greater confidence, knowing that we are part of something far grander and more profound than we can fully understand.

The Echo of Generosity

In the grand theater of existence, every surrounding, every circumstance, stands as a testament to the higher power's boundless generosity and wisdom. Picture the world as an elaborate gift, meticulously crafted and presented with profound thought and care. The beauty of a sunrise, the serenity of a tranquil moment, the challenges that test our resolve—each is a reflection of the divine's infinite grace.

This higher power is the source of every blessing we encounter, from the simplest pleasures to the most profound miracles. The warmth of a loved one's embrace, the comfort of a familiar home, the resilience we find in our darkest hours—these are not mere coincidences or the product of chance. They are the tangible expressions of a divine generosity that permeates every aspect of our lives.

When we come to recognize this truth, we understand that we are not the creators of these gifts but the stewards. We are entrusted with the responsibility to appreciate, nurture, and share the blessings we receive. Our lives become a testament to the divine's wisdom, as we navigate the gifts bestowed upon us with gratitude and purpose.

The recognition that everything we have is a reflection of the higher power's benevolence invites us to live with a sense of reverence and responsibility. It's as if we've been handed a beautiful, fragile artifact and are entrusted with its care. Our actions, our choices, and our gratitude become expressions of our acknowledgment of this divine gift.

Every interaction, every moment of kindness, every decision to embrace life's challenges with grace becomes a way of honoring the divine source from which all blessings flow. In this light, we are reminded that our purpose is not merely to receive but to reflect and amplify this divine generosity in the world around us. By doing so, we honor the higher power's gifts and participate in the ongoing dance of grace and gratitude that defines our existence.

The Art of Letting Go

When we come to understand that everything belongs to the higher power, a profound shift occurs within us. The grip of control and possession that once seemed so crucial begins to loosen. We start to grasp that our attachments—whether to people, possessions, or circumstances—are but fleeting chapters in the grand narrative of life. Each moment, each relationship, is here for a season, intricately woven into a divine orchestration that transcends our immediate understanding.

This realization doesn't mean we abandon care, love, or nurture. On the contrary, it enriches these very experiences. By letting go of the need to control outcomes or possess what we hold dear, we allow ourselves to engage more fully and authentically with the present. We can love deeply without clinging, cherish moments without demanding permanence, and give generously without expecting anything in return.

When we embrace the idea that everything is part of a higher plan, we free ourselves from the burden of trying to dictate every twist and turn. This freedom allows us to experience life with a lighter heart, to appreciate joy without fearing its end, and to navigate loss with a sense of acceptance rather than resistance. Each joy becomes a precious gift to be savored, each loss a poignant reminder of life's transient beauty.

In this light, we can approach life with a sense of grace, knowing that the ebb and flow of experiences are part of a larger, divine design. Our lives become a dance with the cosmos, where we move in harmony with its rhythms rather than struggling against them. We learn to appreciate the beauty of impermanence and the wisdom in trusting the higher power's grand orchestration.

By letting go of the need to control and possess, we open ourselves to a deeper connection with the essence of life. We find peace in the knowledge that, while we are temporary players in this grand drama, every role we undertake contributes to a purpose far greater than ourselves. This acceptance brings a sense of freedom and fulfillment, allowing us to live more fully and with greater appreciation for the transient, yet profoundly meaningful, moments that define our existence.

The Illusion of Choice

In the theater of our lives, the illusion of willpower is a powerful and necessary one. It grants us the sense of purpose and intention, allowing us to navigate through our days with conviction. We believe that our decisions steer the course of our lives, that each choice we make is a testament to our autonomy. Yet, beneath this veneer of control lies a deeper truth: our paths are already charted by the higher power.

Picture life as a grand stage, with every scene and act meticulously planned. We may feel as though we are improvising, making spontaneous decisions at every turn, but the script has been written long before we took our first steps. Even when we stand at a crossroads, agonizing over which direction to take, the outcome is already determined. The higher power has orchestrated each moment, guiding us along a path we may not fully understand but are destined to follow.

This doesn't diminish the value of our experiences or the sincerity of our choices. Rather, it offers a perspective that can bring comfort and clarity. We are participants in a divine drama, playing our roles with the belief that we are the masters of our fate, when in reality, we are actors in a grand production. The choices we make and the struggles we face are part of the beautiful illusion that makes our journey meaningful and rich.

By embracing the idea that our paths are set, we can relinquish some of the pressure and anxiety associated with decision-making. We can approach life's challenges and choices with a sense of ease, knowing that while we may feel the weight of the world on our shoulders, we are ultimately walking a path that has already been paved by a higher hand.

This understanding doesn't negate our responsibility to live with intention and integrity. Instead, it invites us to trust in the greater plan, to appreciate the journey for what it is, and to find peace in the knowledge that we are guided by a force greater than ourselves. In surrendering to this divine orchestration, we discover a profound sense of freedom and serenity, knowing that our lives are unfolding exactly as they are meant to.

The Divine Design of Obstacles

Every obstacle we encounter, every setback that disrupts our path, carries with it a purpose far greater than we often realize. Life, with all its twists and turns, is not a random series of events. Each challenge is placed before us by the higher power, not as a punishment or a test of our worth, but as a deliberate step in shaping who we are meant to become. These moments of hardship, confusion, and frustration are tools in the hands of the divine, chiseling away at the rough edges of our character and moving us closer to the fulfillment of His purpose for our lives.

When we face difficulties, it is easy to become overwhelmed by the immediate discomfort they cause. We worry about outcomes, fearing that we may lose something precious or miss an opportunity. Yet, if we step back and view these obstacles from a higher perspective, we begin to see them not as roadblocks, but as carefully designed markers along our journey—each one serving a greater good, even if that good is not immediately apparent.

The higher power doesn't place obstacles in our way to watch us struggle aimlessly. Instead, these challenges are carefully calibrated to teach us valuable lessons: patience, resilience, humility, or faith. They push us beyond our comfort zones, urging us to grow in ways we might not have chosen for ourselves. And often, the struggles we face today are preparing us for the victories of tomorrow.

When we trust in the higher power's wisdom and embrace the belief that everything is happening exactly as it should, we release ourselves from the burden of fear and doubt. We no longer feel the need to control every outcome because we understand that the divine is already in control. Each setback is not a failure, but a redirection, guiding us toward a higher purpose that we may not yet fully comprehend.

This trust in the higher power's design allows us to navigate life's storms with a sense of peace. Instead of seeing obstacles as threats, we begin to recognize them as opportunities for growth, perfectly placed to lead us closer to our divine destiny. It is in this surrender to the flow of life that we find true strength, knowing that even in the face of adversity, we are being carried forward by a force far greater than ourselves.

The Eternal Companion

When you find yourself in the depths of despair, feeling deserted and destroyed, remember this simple, yet profound truth: you are never truly alone. The higher power, the force behind all creation, is not just a distant deity or an abstract concept. He is your eternal companion, intricately woven into every fiber of your existence.

His love is an ever-present embrace, surrounding you with warmth and comfort even when you feel isolated. In moments of darkness, when hope seems like a distant memory, His presence is there, sustaining you with a quiet, steadfast assurance. It is a love that does not falter or waver, even when you are at your lowest, when the weight of the world feels unbearable.

The higher power's plan is working through every challenge you face, guiding you through the trials and tribulations of life. Every hardship, every setback, is not a sign of abandonment but a part of the divine plan, meticulously designed to lead you to a place of growth and fulfillment. Even when the path seems obscured and the journey feels interminable, know that you are being guided forward, step by step, by a force that is both powerful and profoundly loving.

In your moments of deepest struggle, take solace in the knowledge that you are cherished beyond measure. The higher power's guidance is gentle yet unwavering, holding you close and reminding you that you are never truly alone. His presence is the light that pierces through the darkness, the whisper of reassurance in the silence, the unyielding support that carries you through.

So, when you feel lost and broken, hold on to this truth: you are enveloped in divine love, and you are always, always cherished. Even in your lowest moments, remember that the higher power is there, your eternal companion, guiding you with a hand of grace and an embrace of unconditional love.

The Unfolding Journey

In the bleakest hours of life, when it feels as though time is slipping away and hope has vanished, it's tempting to believe that your journey has reached its final chapter. You might find yourself convinced that the end of the road is in sight, that your best days are behind you, and that any sense of purpose has long since faded. Yet, in these moments of profound despair, it is crucial to hold fast to one powerful truth: the grand plan crafted by the higher power for your life is still unfolding.

Your story is not over; it is merely entering a new phase. The darkness you experience is not an end but a transition—a temporary shadow that precedes a new dawn. The higher power, with infinite wisdom and foresight, is still at work in your life, weaving together the threads of your experiences into a tapestry of profound beauty and purpose.

Think of these dark moments as a pause in a symphony, a deep breath before the crescendo. Just as the most stirring melodies often follow the quietest interludes, so too do your greatest triumphs often arise from the depths of your struggles. The grand plan is not static but dynamic, continuously evolving and expanding as you grow and change.

In these times of feeling lost or defeated, remind yourself that the journey is ongoing, and the higher power's hand is guiding you through every twist and turn. The end you fear is not an end at all but a gateway to new beginnings. Each challenge you face, each moment of doubt, is a part of the larger narrative that is shaping you into the person you are meant to become.

Your story is still being written, and every chapter, no matter how difficult, is contributing to a greater whole. Embrace the uncertainty with faith, knowing that the higher power's plan encompasses not just the present but the entirety of your journey. The most remarkable developments often come from the darkest places, and your best days are yet to come.

So, when you find yourself at the edge of despair, remember that the higher power is still guiding your path. Your story is not finished—it's only just beginning. Hold on to the promise of new beginnings and trust in the unfolding of a grand plan that is far beyond your immediate sight. The journey continues, and with it, the potential for renewal, growth, and extraordinary purpose.

Embracing His Constant Companionship

In moments of distress and loneliness, when the weight of the world seems unbearable and every step feels like a struggle, it's natural to feel as though you are facing your challenges entirely alone. The darkness of these times can make it hard to see beyond your immediate pain, creating a sense of isolation that feels all-encompassing. Yet, even in these moments of profound distress, it's crucial to remember that you are never truly alone. The higher power's constant companionship is with you, even when His presence seems elusive.

Here's how to navigate these difficult times with the assurance of His unending support:

Acknowledge the Presence: Begin by acknowledging that the higher power is with you, even if you can't feel His presence directly. This recognition is a powerful first step in shifting your perspective from isolation to connection. Take a moment to breathe deeply and remind yourself that you are encompassed by a love that transcends all understanding.

Find Solace in Reflection: Reflect on past moments when you felt guided or comforted in ways you didn't fully understand at the time. These reflections can serve as reminders of the higher power's ongoing influence in your life. Journaling or meditating on these experiences can help reinforce the idea that you are never truly alone.

Seek Comfort in Faith: Lean into your faith or spiritual practices during these times. Whether through prayer, meditation, or reading sacred texts, these practices can provide a sense of connection and solace. They act as channels through which you can feel the higher power's presence more acutely and receive comfort.

Reach Out for Support: Sometimes, experiencing the higher power's companionship can also come through the support of others. Reach out to friends, family, or spiritual advisors who can offer comfort, understanding, and a reminder of the divine support that surrounds you. Human connections can often become conduits for experiencing the higher power's love and care.

Embrace the Stillness: In the midst of chaos and emotional turmoil, create moments of stillness and quiet. Allow yourself to be present with your thoughts and emotions without judgment. In these moments of calm, you may find a deeper awareness of the higher power's presence and a renewed sense of inner peace.

Practice Gratitude: Even when it feels difficult, practice gratitude for the small things in life. This practice shifts your focus from what is troubling you to what is still good and meaningful. Gratitude can open your heart to recognizing the subtle ways in which the higher power is present in your life.

Trust in the Divine Plan: Trust that the higher power is working through every aspect of your life, including your struggles. Believing in a divine plan can provide reassurance that there is purpose and direction even in times of hardship. Embrace the notion that your current distress is a part of a greater journey, one that is being guided by a loving and wise force.

By embracing these practices, you align yourself with the higher power's constant companionship, even when it feels hidden or distant. Remember, His presence is unwavering and omnipresent, a steady beacon in the tumultuous sea of your experiences. In times of distress and loneliness, turn inward and outward with faith, seeking and finding comfort in the enduring support of the higher power who is always, always with you.

Navigating Moments of Doubt

Even the most steadfast believers may face moments of doubt when the existence of the higher power seems uncertain. These periods of questioning can feel unsettling and can shake the very foundation of your faith. However, it is crucial to recognize that doubt is a natural part of the faith journey, not a sign of failure or weakness. Here's how to navigate these challenging moments and reaffirm your connection with the divine:

Acknowledge Your Doubts: Accepting that doubt is a normal part of the spiritual journey is the first step in addressing it. Recognize your feelings without judgment and understand that questioning can be a path to deeper faith and understanding. By acknowledging your doubts, you create space for exploration and growth.

Engage in Open Dialogue: Speak openly about your doubts with a trusted friend, mentor, or spiritual advisor. Engaging in honest conversations about your struggles can provide new perspectives and insights. Sometimes, discussing your doubts can help clarify your thoughts and reinforce your belief.

Seek Spiritual Reflection: Delve into your spiritual practices with renewed intention. Reading sacred texts, engaging in prayer or meditation, and reflecting on the teachings of your faith can offer reassurance and clarity. These practices can help ground you in the wisdom and presence of the higher power.

Remember Past Experiences: Reflect on previous instances when you felt the presence of the higher power in your life. Consider moments of profound connection, guidance, or comfort that have shaped your faith. Recalling these experiences can remind you of the higher power's influence and support, even when it feels distant.

Explore the Meaning of Doubt: Consider what your doubt is teaching you. Sometimes, doubt can reveal areas where your understanding needs to grow or where your faith might need to be re-examined. Embrace the opportunity to deepen your knowledge and relationship with the divine.

Practice Patience with Yourself: Understand that faith is a journey, not a destination. It's okay to have periods of uncertainty and to question your beliefs. Be patient with yourself as you navigate these moments, knowing that they are a part of the larger process of spiritual growth.

Find Comfort in Community: Surround yourself with a supportive faith community. Being part of a group that shares your beliefs can offer encouragement and remind you of the collective strength and faith. Community support can be a source of inspiration and renewal during times of doubt.

Embrace the Mystery: Recognize that some aspects of the divine are beyond human comprehension. Embracing the mystery of the higher power can be a way to accept and appreciate the limitations of our understanding. Trust that there is a greater plan and that not all questions will have immediate answers.

Act in Faith: Even when you feel uncertain, continue to act in accordance with your beliefs and values. Engaging in acts of kindness, service, and compassion can reinforce your connection with the higher power and remind you of the impact of living out your faith.

Allow Time for Renewal: Give yourself permission to take time for reflection and renewal. Sometimes, stepping away from intense questioning and engaging in activities that bring you joy and peace can provide a fresh perspective and renewed sense of connection.

Navigating moments of doubt requires patience, openness, and a willingness to explore the deeper dimensions of your faith. By embracing these practices, you can reaffirm your connection with the higher power and find strength in the journey, even when the path seems uncertain. Trust that doubt, though challenging, is a part of the spiritual journey that can lead to a more profound and resilient faith.

Trusting in His Provision

In moments of uncertainty and need, it can be challenging to maintain faith that the higher power will provide for you. Yet, trust in His provision is essential for nurturing a deep and unwavering connection with the divine. Just as He meticulously created the world with care and intention, so too does He tend to your needs with the same level of attention. Here's how to cultivate trust in His provision and strengthen your faith in His ability to deliver what is best for you:

Acknowledge His Provision: Begin by acknowledging that the higher power is aware of your needs and is committed to providing for you. Trust that His wisdom surpasses your own understanding and that His timing is perfect. Embrace the belief that He knows what is best for you and will deliver accordingly, even if it may not align with your immediate desires or expectations.

Reflect on Past Provisions: Take time to look back at moments in your life when you experienced unexpected support or blessings. These instances are tangible reminders of the higher power's ability to provide. Reflecting on how you have been cared for in the past can reinforce your trust in His continued provision. Consider writing these reflections in a journal to create a record of His faithfulness that you can turn to during times of doubt.

Cultivate Gratitude: Develop a practice of gratitude by regularly acknowledging and appreciating the blessings you experience daily. Whether it's the support of loved ones, opportunities that arise, or simple moments of joy, recognizing these as gifts from the higher power helps reinforce His role as the source of all good in your life. Gratitude transforms your perspective, highlighting His ongoing provision and fostering a closer relationship with Him.

Trust in His Timing: Understand that the higher power's timing may differ from your own. Patience is key as you await His provision. Trust that He is working behind the scenes, orchestrating events in ways that you might not immediately see or understand. Embrace the belief that His timing is always aligned with what is best for you.

Pray for Guidance: Engage in prayer, asking the higher power for guidance and strength as you wait for His provision. Prayer is a way to communicate your needs and desires, while also expressing your trust in His plan. It can be a source of comfort and reassurance as you navigate periods of uncertainty.

Act in Faith: Live your life with faith in His provision, even when things seem uncertain. Acting with faith means continuing to move forward, making decisions, and pursuing opportunities while trusting that the higher power will provide what is necessary. Your actions can reflect your belief in His ability to meet your needs.

Seek Support from Others: Surround yourself with a supportive community that can offer encouragement and reminders of the higher power's provision. Sharing your journey with others can provide additional perspectives and reinforce your faith in His care.

Embrace the Journey: Understand that trust in His provision is a journey, not a destination. It involves continually learning to rely on His wisdom and timing, even when faced with challenges. Embrace this journey with an open heart and a willingness to grow in your faith.

By embracing these practices, you strengthen your trust in the higher power's provision and deepen your connection with Him. Remember that He is attentive to your needs, providing with care and intention. Trust in His timing and wisdom, and allow your faith to guide you through every moment of need and uncertainty.

Trusting in His Provision

In moments of uncertainty and need, it can be challenging to maintain faith that the higher power will provide for you. Yet, trust in His provision is essential for nurturing a deep and unwavering connection with the divine. Just as He meticulously created the world with care and intention, so too does He tend to your needs with the same level of attention. Here's how to cultivate trust in His provision and strengthen your faith in His ability to deliver what is best for you:

Acknowledge His Provision: Begin by acknowledging that the higher power is aware of your needs and is committed to providing for you. Trust that His wisdom surpasses your own understanding and that His timing is perfect. Embrace the belief that He knows what is best for you and will deliver accordingly, even if it may not align with your immediate desires or expectations.

Reflect on Past Provisions: Take time to look back at moments in your life when you experienced unexpected support or blessings. These instances are tangible reminders of the higher power's ability to provide. Reflecting on how you have been cared for in the past can reinforce your trust in His continued provision. Consider writing these reflections in a journal to create a record of His faithfulness that you can turn to during times of doubt.

Cultivate Gratitude: Develop a practice of gratitude by regularly acknowledging and appreciating the blessings you experience daily. Whether it's the support of loved ones, opportunities that arise, or simple moments of joy, recognizing these as gifts from the higher power helps reinforce His role as the source of all good in your life. Gratitude transforms your perspective, highlighting His ongoing provision and fostering a closer relationship with Him.

Trust in His Timing: Understand that the higher power's timing may differ from your own. Patience is key as you await His provision. Trust that He is working behind the scenes, orchestrating events in ways that you might not immediately see or understand. Embrace the belief that His timing is always aligned with what is best for you.

Pray for Guidance: Engage in prayer, asking the higher power for guidance and strength as you wait for His provision. Prayer is a way to communicate your needs and desires, while also expressing your trust in His plan. It can be a source of comfort and reassurance as you navigate periods of uncertainty.

Act in Faith: Live your life with faith in His provision, even when things seem uncertain. Acting with faith means continuing to move forward, making decisions, and pursuing opportunities while trusting that the higher power will provide what is necessary. Your actions can reflect your belief in His ability to meet your needs.

Embrace a Mindset of Abundance: Adopt a mindset that sees abundance rather than scarcity. The higher power's resources are limitless, and His ability to provide extends beyond human comprehension. Embracing this perspective can help you feel more secure and hopeful, knowing that there is always more available than you might initially perceive. Trust that His provision is not constrained by limitations but flows from an infinite source.

Embrace the Journey: Understand that trust in His provision is a journey, not a destination. It involves continually learning to rely on His wisdom and timing, even when faced with challenges. Embrace this journey with an open heart and a willingness to grow in your faith.

By embracing these practices, you strengthen your trust in the higher power's provision and deepen your connection with Him. Remember that He is attentive to your needs, providing with care and intention. Trust in His timing, wisdom, and limitless resources, and allow your faith to guide you through every moment of need and uncertainty.

Recognizing the Divine in the Everyday

In the ebb and flow of daily life, it's easy to overlook the subtle ways the higher power is present. Amidst the rush and routine of everyday activities, His divine presence may seem distant or invisible. Yet, He is with you in every minute moment, providing guidance, support, and sustenance through the smallest details and ordinary occurrences. This divine presence isn't confined to grand events or significant milestones; it extends to the seemingly mundane and routine aspects of life. Here's how to recognize and appreciate His presence in the everyday:

Pay Attention to the Small Things: Notice the little details that make up your daily life. From a smile from a stranger to a moment of unexpected peace, these small events can be seen as expressions of the higher power's presence. By paying attention to these subtle signs, you open yourself to recognizing His constant involvement in your life.

Find Meaning in Routine Tasks: Even the most ordinary tasks, like cooking a meal or commuting to work, can be infused with a sense of purpose and connection to the divine. Approach these routines with mindfulness and gratitude, acknowledging that they are opportunities to experience His provision and care in everyday activities.

Reflect on Daily Blessings: Take time each day to reflect on the blessings you have received, no matter how small. These can be moments of joy, comfort, or support that might otherwise go unnoticed. By reflecting on these daily blessings, you can recognize the higher power's hand in the everyday aspects of your life.

Practice Mindfulness: Engage in mindfulness practices to become more aware of the present moment. Mindfulness can help you attune to the divine presence that permeates even the simplest experiences. By being fully present, you can better appreciate the subtle ways the higher power interacts with your life.

Express Gratitude for the Everyday: Develop a habit of expressing gratitude for the small, daily gifts and experiences. Whether it's a beautiful sunset, a kind word from a friend, or a moment of rest, acknowledging these blessings helps you recognize the higher power's ongoing involvement in your life.

See the Divine in Relationships: Recognize that your interactions with others can be a reflection of the divine presence. The love, support, and compassion you experience in relationships are manifestations of the higher power working through people. Appreciate these connections as expressions of His care and guidance.

Embrace the Rhythm of Life: Understand that life has its natural rhythms, including times of activity and rest, success and struggle. Trust that the higher power is present in every phase, providing balance and support. Embrace the flow of life with the awareness that His guidance is present in every shift and change.

Find Joy in the Ordinary: Allow yourself to find joy and contentment in the ordinary moments of life. Whether it's enjoying a cup of coffee, reading a book, or taking a walk, these moments can be seen as opportunities to connect with the divine. Embracing joy in the ordinary helps you recognize His presence in all aspects of life.

Share Your Experiences: Talk about the small ways you experience the divine presence with others. Sharing your observations and experiences can reinforce your awareness and encourage others to recognize the higher power's involvement in their own lives.

Stay Open to Surprises: Be open to unexpected ways the higher power might manifest in your daily life. Sometimes, the divine presence can be revealed through surprising or unconventional means. By staying open to these possibilities, you allow yourself to be more attuned to the higher power's subtle guidance and support.

By incorporating these practices into your daily life, you cultivate a deeper awareness of the divine presence in the everyday. Recognize that the higher power's involvement extends to every detail, routine, and interaction. Embracing this awareness enhances your connection with the divine and brings a sense of meaning and gratitude to every moment.

Rising Above Adversity with Divine Guidance

In times of challenge and conflict, when it feels like obstacles are overwhelming and adversaries are relentless, it's essential to hold firm in the belief that the higher power is there to lift you above your enemies. His guidance and strength are unwavering, ensuring that you rise above adversity and emerge victorious. Here's how to draw upon His divine support to overcome the fiercest of trials and navigate conflicts with courage and resilience:

Embrace Divine Strength: Recognize that the higher power is a source of immense strength and resilience. In moments when you feel weak or defeated, call upon His strength to empower you. Trust that His presence provides the fortitude needed to face and overcome challenges. Your belief in His support can turn moments of weakness into opportunities for demonstrating inner strength.

See Obstacles as Opportunities: Understand that the higher power can transform obstacles into opportunities for growth and victory. Each challenge you face is a chance to develop new skills, gain insight, and build character. Embrace difficulties as part of the divine plan, knowing that they are designed to elevate you and help you grow.

Trust in His Plan: Have faith that the higher power's plan for you encompasses not only your triumphs but also the means to achieve them. When faced with adversaries, trust that His guidance will lead you through the conflict and toward a resolution that aligns with His greater purpose for your life. Your confidence in His plan can provide clarity and direction amidst uncertainty.

Seek Guidance Through Prayer: In moments of conflict, turn to prayer for guidance and strength. Prayer is a way to connect with the higher power, seek His support, and gain insight into how to navigate your challenges. Use prayer as a tool to ask for courage, wisdom, and clarity in confronting your adversaries.

Draw on Inner Resilience: Remember that the higher power has endowed you with inner resilience and strength. Even when external circumstances seem daunting, trust in your own capacity to endure and rise above. The divine presence within you fortifies your ability to face and overcome obstacles.

Find Courage in His Presence: When facing difficulties, draw courage from the knowledge that you are never alone. The higher power's presence is with you, providing comfort and reassurance. This awareness can instill a sense of bravery and determination as you confront and overcome your adversaries.

Embrace Divine Timing: Trust that the higher power's timing is perfect and that He is working behind the scenes to bring about a resolution. Be patient and stay steadfast in your faith, knowing that His plan will unfold in its own time. Embrace the process and remain confident that you are being guided toward victory.

Learn from Each Challenge: View each challenge as a lesson in divine guidance and strength. Reflect on what you learn through adversity and how these lessons contribute to your growth. Understanding that each trial has a purpose can help you maintain perspective and find meaning in difficult experiences.

Celebrate Victories: Acknowledge and celebrate your victories, no matter how small they may seem. Recognizing the role of the higher power in your achievements reinforces your belief in His guidance and support. Celebrating these moments strengthens your faith and encourages you to continue facing future challenges with confidence.

By drawing on the higher power's guidance and strength, you can navigate conflicts and adversities with resilience and courage. Trust in His ability to lift you above your enemies and transform obstacles into opportunities for growth. Embrace His divine plan, seek His support through prayer, and find strength in His unwavering presence. As you rise above your challenges, you will emerge stronger and more empowered, reflecting the higher power's transformative influence in your life.

Placing the Higher Power Above All

For the higher power to guide you to true victory, there is one essential truth: you must place Him above everything and everyone in your life. This profound act of surrendering fully to His will and acknowledging that nothing else—no person, no material possession, no worldly ambition—holds greater importance than His presence and purpose is the key to experiencing divine guidance and success. Here's how to embrace this truth and align your life with the higher power's supreme influence:

Surrender to Divine Will: **To place the higher power above all else, you must first surrender to His will. This means letting go of your own plans and desires, and trusting that His purpose for you is greater and more fulfilling than anything you could create on your own. Surrendering involves accepting His guidance and being open to the path He has laid out for you, even when it diverges from your own expectations.

Prioritize His Presence: Make the higher power's presence the central focus of your life. This involves prioritizing your relationship with Him above all other relationships and commitments. Spend time in prayer, meditation, and reflection to strengthen your connection with Him. By placing His presence at the core of your life, you invite His influence into every decision and action.

Release Attachments to the Temporary: Recognize that material possessions and worldly ambitions are temporary and cannot provide the lasting fulfillment or security that the higher power offers. Release your attachment to these transient things and shift your focus to the eternal and unchanging presence of the divine. This shift in perspective allows you to find true contentment and stability in His guidance.

Align Your Actions with His Purpose: Let the higher power's purpose guide your actions and decisions. Evaluate your goals and ambitions in light of His will, and adjust them as needed to align with His plan. By ensuring that your actions are in harmony with His purpose, you open yourself to receiving His support and guidance in achieving true victory.

Trust in Divine Timing: Understand that placing the higher power above all involves trusting in His timing. Recognize that His plans may unfold differently from your expectations, and that His timing is perfect. Patience and trust in His process allow you to remain steadfast and confident, even when immediate results are not apparent.

Find Strength in His Presence: When facing challenges, draw strength from the higher power's presence. Knowing that He is above all things provides a sense of security and courage. In times of difficulty, remind yourself that His power is greater than any obstacle you may encounter, and that He is guiding you toward victory.

Cultivate a Spirit of Gratitude: Foster a spirit of gratitude for the higher power's presence and guidance in your life. Acknowledge His role in your successes and challenges, and express appreciation for His support. Gratitude reinforces your connection with Him and reinforces the importance of placing Him above all else.

Live with Purpose and Integrity: Align your daily life with the higher power's principles and values. Live with purpose and integrity, reflecting His teachings in your actions and interactions. By embodying His principles, you demonstrate your commitment to placing Him at the center of your life.

Seek His Guidance in All Things: Make a habit of seeking the higher power's guidance in all aspects of your life. Whether facing decisions, challenges, or opportunities, turn to Him for insight and direction. By consistently seeking His input, you reinforce His position as the ultimate authority and source of guidance.

Encourage Others to Follow: Share the message of placing the higher power above all with others. Encourage those around you to recognize His supreme influence and to prioritize His presence in their own lives. By leading by example and offering support, you help create a community that values and honors the divine above all else.

By placing the higher power above everything and everyone, you open yourself to His divine influence and guidance. This act of surrender and prioritization allows

His presence to reign supreme in your life, leading you to true victory and fulfillment. Embrace the path of placing Him first, and experience the transformative power of His guidance in every aspect of your journey.

Centering Your Life Around Faith: Finding True Peace

In the quest for meaning and fulfillment, deepening your connection with the higher power is the only pursuit that truly matters. When your life is anchored in faith, the opinions, judgments, and expectations of others lose their power over you. Instead, you find a profound peace in knowing that you are living in alignment with the divine plan. Here's how to center your life around your faith and discover the true peace that comes from this alignment:

Prioritize Daily Devotion: Make time each day to connect with the higher power through prayer, meditation, or reflection. Establishing a regular practice helps deepen your relationship with Him and keeps your faith at the forefront of your life. These moments of devotion are essential for nurturing your spiritual connection and maintaining focus on what truly matters.

Align Your Actions with Faith: Let your faith guide your actions and decisions. When you center your life around your connection with the higher power, you make choices that reflect His teachings and values. This alignment brings a sense of purpose and clarity, allowing you to *navigate life with confidence and integrity.*

Release External Validation: Recognize that the approval or disapproval of others is secondary to the divine plan. As you deepen your connection with the higher power, the need for external validation diminishes. Focus on living authentically according to His will, rather than seeking approval from others.

Find Peace in Alignment: Embrace the peace that comes from living in alignment with the divine plan. When your life is centered around your faith, you experience a deep sense of inner tranquility. This peace is not dependent on external circumstances but is a reflection of your harmony with the higher power's purpose for your life.

Trust in Divine Wisdom: Trust that the higher power's wisdom surpasses your own understanding. When you center your life around faith, you acknowledge that His guidance is superior to any advice or opinions you might receive from others. Trust in His plan and timing, and find comfort in His wisdom.

Embrace Faith Over Fear: In moments of doubt or fear, turn to your faith for strength and reassurance. When your connection with the higher power is your primary focus, you are less likely to be swayed by fear or uncertainty. Embrace the courage that comes from knowing that you are supported and guided by a higher force.

Cultivate Inner Strength: Deepening your connection with the higher power fosters inner strength and resilience. As you center your life around faith, you develop a sense of empowerment that comes from knowing you are part of a greater divine plan. This strength helps you face challenges with grace and determination.

Live with Purpose: Allow your faith to define your sense of purpose. When your life is centered around the higher power, you find meaning in living according to His will. This purpose provides direction and motivation, helping you to live a life that is fulfilling and aligned with divine intentions.

Let Go of Control: Surrender the illusion of control and trust in the higher power's plan. When you focus on deepening your connection with Him, you release the need to control every aspect of your life. This surrender allows you to embrace the flow of His plan and find peace in His guidance.

Share Your Faith Journey: Inspire others by sharing your journey of faith and the peace you have found through it. Your example can encourage those around you to deepen their own connection with the higher power and center their lives around faith. By sharing your experiences, you contribute to a community of spiritual growth and support.

By focusing on deepening your connection with the higher power, you shift your priorities away from external judgments and towards what truly matters. This shift brings a profound peace that comes from living in alignment with the divine plan. Embrace this journey of faith, and find fulfillment in knowing that nothing else holds greater importance than your relationship with the higher power.

Embracing Misfortunes as Divine Unfolding

In the face of misfortunes and challenges, it's natural to question why such difficulties occur. Rather than viewing these trials as punishment or meaningless chaos, recognize them as integral parts of the divine unfolding. The higher power is not distant or indifferent in your pain; instead, He is with you, guiding you through every storm and leading you toward brighter horizons. Here's how to shift your perspective and find meaning in the midst of adversity:

Reframe Misfortunes as Divine Guidance: Understand that misfortunes are not arbitrary or punitive but are woven into the fabric of a greater divine plan. Each challenge you face is an opportunity for growth, learning, and alignment with the higher power's purpose. Reframe these experiences as guidance rather than punishment.

Seek the Hidden Lessons: In moments of difficulty, look for the lessons that the higher power may be imparting. Ask yourself what you can learn from the situation and how it can contribute to your personal and spiritual development. Trust that there is a reason behind the struggle, even if it is not immediately clear.

Trust in Divine Love: Remember that the higher power's presence is unwavering, even in your darkest moments. His love surrounds you, providing comfort and strength. Trust that His plan for you is rooted in love, and that every hardship is an opportunity for you to grow closer to Him.

Embrace Growth Through Adversity: Recognize that challenges and misfortunes often lead to significant personal and spiritual growth. Embrace these experiences as necessary steps in your journey toward becoming who you are meant to be. The higher power uses adversity to shape and strengthen you.

Practice Patience and Faith: Cultivate patience and faith in the midst of trials. Trust that the higher power's plan is unfolding in its own time and that every hardship has a purpose. By practicing patience and maintaining faith, you align yourself with the divine flow and find solace in His guidance.

Find Strength in His Presence: Lean on the higher power for strength and support during difficult times. His presence provides the courage and resilience needed to navigate through challenges. When you feel overwhelmed, turn to Him for solace and strength.

Keep a Broader Perspective: Understand that the current difficulty is part of a larger picture that may not be immediately visible. The higher power's plan encompasses a broader perspective, and what seems like chaos now may be a small piece of a grand and purposeful design.

Affirm Your Faith Through Prayer: Use prayer to reaffirm your faith and seek comfort. In your prayers, express your trust in the higher power's plan and ask for His guidance through the current trial. Prayer strengthens your connection with Him and helps you find peace amidst the struggle.

Celebrate Small Victories: Acknowledge and celebrate small victories and moments of clarity that arise from your struggles. Each step forward, no matter how minor, is a sign of progress and a testament to the higher power's guidance.

By shifting your perspective and embracing misfortunes as part of the divine unfolding, you align yourself with a higher purpose and find meaning in your trials. Trust that the higher power is with you, guiding you through the storm and leading you toward a brighter future. Even when the reasons behind your struggles are not clear, have faith that they are rooted in love, growth, and His greater plan for you.

Trusting When Prayers Seem Unanswered

There are moments in life when your prayers seem to go unheard, when your deepest desires and needs remain unmet despite your heartfelt pleas. In these moments, it's easy to feel discouraged or abandoned. However, it's crucial to remember that the higher power hears every word, every plea, and every whisper of your soul. Even when it seems like He is silent, He is working on your behalf in ways that may not be immediately visible.

Here are some ways to strengthen your faith when your prayers seem unanswered:

Understand Divine Timing: Often, when prayers seem unanswered, it is not because the higher power is saying "no" but because He is saying "not yet." There is a divine timing at work, one that operates beyond our understanding. Trust that the higher power's timing is perfect, and that what you seek will come when it is meant to—at the time that is most aligned with your highest good.

Believe in a Higher Plan: Trust that the higher power always has a greater plan for you, one that may differ from your own expectations. What you are praying for might not be in line with that plan, or there may be something even better waiting for you. Believe that every prayer is acknowledged and that the higher power is working in ways that serve your best interests, even if you cannot see it yet.

Let Go of Expectations: Release the need for your prayers to be answered in a specific way. The higher power's wisdom surpasses human understanding, and sometimes the answer to your prayers may come in a form you did not expect. By letting go of rigid expectations, you open yourself to receiving blessings in new and unexpected ways.

Find Comfort in Patience: Cultivate patience, knowing that the higher power is working behind the scenes. It can be difficult to wait, especially when you are in distress, but patience allows you to stay aligned with divine timing.

In moments of waiting, find solace in the knowledge that the higher power has heard your prayers and is preparing the path ahead.

Trust in His Presence: Even when prayers seem unanswered, know that the higher power is with you. His presence surrounds you at all times, and His love is constant. Trust that He is guiding you, even through the silence, and that He will never leave you to walk your journey alone.

Recognize Unseen Answers: Sometimes, answers to prayers come in ways that are not immediately apparent. Take time to reflect on your life and consider whether the higher power has already provided in subtle or indirect ways. A shift in your mindset, a new opportunity, or an unexpected blessing might be the answer you've been seeking.

Strengthen Your Faith Through Reflection: Reflect on past moments when you thought your prayers went unanswered, only to later realize that the higher power had something better planned for you. Use these experiences as reminders that His plan is always in motion, even when it is not obvious at the time.

Pray for Strength and Clarity: When your prayers seem unanswered, focus your prayers on seeking strength, clarity, and peace rather than solely on the desired outcome. By praying for guidance through the uncertainty, you align yourself with the higher power's will and find comfort in His presence.

Embrace Gratitude for the Journey: Be grateful for the journey, even when it takes unexpected turns. Every experience, whether it feels like an answered prayer or not, is part of the divine plan. Gratitude helps you stay open to the lessons and blessings that come your way, regardless of how they manifest.

Maintain Hope and Trust: Hold on to hope and trust in the higher power's plan for your life. Even when it feels like nothing is happening, remember that the higher power is always working on your behalf. His plans for you are rooted in love and wisdom, and He will provide what is best for you in due time.

When your prayers seem unanswered, don't lose heart. Know that every prayer is heard and acknowledged, and that the higher power's response may be "not yet" or "I have something better planned." Trust in His timing, wisdom, and love, and remember that the divine plan for your life is always unfolding—sometimes in ways you never imagined, but always with your highest good in mind.

Letting Go of Regret

Regret can be a heavy burden, often weighing us down with thoughts of missed opportunities and past mistakes. It's a relentless reminder of what could have been, clouding our present and future with a sense of sorrow and frustration. However, embracing the notion that everything unfolds according to a divine plan can provide a profound shift in perspective, helping us release the grip of regret and find peace.

Letting go of regret begins with acknowledging that the past cannot be changed. It is easy to get caught up in "what ifs" and "if onlys," but such thoughts only serve to anchor us to a time that no longer exists. Recognizing that each moment has led us to where we are today is crucial. Every choice, every misstep, has contributed to our growth and the unfolding of our life's journey.

Embracing the belief that there is a higher power guiding us can transform how we view our past. The higher power's plan encompasses all our experiences, including the moments we regret. It suggests that our missteps are not merely failures but integral parts of a grand design that shapes who we are meant to become. Trusting in this plan allows us to see our past not as a series of mistakes but as a tapestry of experiences that contribute to our unique path.

Rather than dwelling on the past, focus on the lessons learned and the ways you have grown. Regret often stems from a lack of understanding or acceptance of our past actions. By reflecting on the growth that has emerged from these experiences, we begin to see that our past is not a source of shame but a testament to our resilience and capacity for change.

Forgiveness is also a vital aspect of letting go of regret. This includes forgiving yourself for past mistakes and understanding that everyone makes errors. The higher power's grace and compassion extend to us, and embracing this can help us extend the same grace to ourselves. Self-forgiveness allows us to release the burden of regret and move forward with a renewed sense of purpose and self-compassion.

Living in the present moment is another powerful way to overcome regret. By fully engaging with the here and now, we shift our focus from what has been lost to what is currently available to us. Each moment presents a new opportunity to make choices aligned with our values and goals. Embracing the present helps us to break free from the past's constraints and build a future grounded in intentionality and hope.

Moreover, placing trust in the higher power's guidance can offer solace when regret arises. Believing that there is a divine reason for everything that has happened can help us release the need to control outcomes and accept that the higher power is steering us toward our ultimate good. This trust fosters a sense of peace, knowing that our past is part of a larger, benevolent plan.

To truly let go of regret, it's essential to cultivate a mindset of gratitude. By focusing on what you have rather than what you have lost, you can shift your perspective. Gratitude for the lessons learned, the growth achieved, and the opportunities that lie ahead helps to transform regret into a source of strength and motivation.

Ultimately, letting go of regret is about embracing the journey of life with all its ups and downs, knowing that each experience contributes to the person you are becoming. Trust in the higher power's plan allows you to release the weight of regret, find peace in the present, and move forward with hope and confidence. By doing so, you honor the divine design of your life and open yourself to the endless possibilities that lie ahead.

Overcoming Fear: Trusting the Higher Power's Plan

Fear is a powerful force, often paralyzing us and keeping us from embracing the fullness of life. It manifests in various forms—fear of the unknown, fear of failure, fear of loss. However, finding solace in the belief that a higher power is watching over us and guiding our steps can transform our approach to fear and empower us to face life's challenges with courage and confidence.

The first step in overcoming fear is to recognize that it is a natural part of the human experience. Fear often arises when we encounter uncertainty or perceive a threat, but it doesn't have to dictate our actions or define our reality. Understanding that fear is a response, not a permanent state, allows us to begin addressing it from a place of empowerment rather than helplessness.

Trusting in the higher power's protection is key to alleviating fear. Believing that there is a divine force guiding and safeguarding us can provide a profound sense of security. When you feel overwhelmed by fear, remind yourself that you are not alone; the higher power's presence envelops you, offering strength and reassurance. This trust can help shift your focus from what could go wrong to the support and guidance that is constantly available to you.

Recognizing that there is a divine plan at work helps to put fear into perspective. The higher power's plan encompasses all aspects of your life, including the challenges and uncertainties you face. Trusting that this plan is designed with your highest good in mind can alleviate fear by shifting your focus from immediate concerns to the broader, more reassuring view of life's purpose. Even in moments of fear, you can find comfort in the knowledge that there is a greater design at play, leading you toward your ultimate good.

Facing fear often requires taking action despite feeling afraid. Courage is not the absence of fear but the ability to move forward in spite of it. By taking steps toward your goals, you align with the higher power's plan and demonstrate your trust in the divine guidance available to you. Each step taken, no matter how small, reinforces your ability to confront and overcome fear.

Another powerful way to overcome fear is through prayer and meditation. These practices allow you to connect with the higher power, seek comfort, and find inner peace. In moments of fear, turning to prayer can help center your thoughts and remind you of the higher power's protective presence. Meditation provides a space to quiet the mind and focus on the assurance that you are supported and guided.

Building a strong support system also plays a crucial role in managing fear. Surrounding yourself with compassionate, understanding individuals can provide encouragement and perspective. These connections remind you that you are not alone and that there are others who can offer support and guidance as you navigate through fearful situations.

It is also helpful to confront and challenge the root causes of your fear. Often, fear is based on misconceptions or past experiences rather than present realities. By examining the sources of your fear, you can address them directly and reframe your perspective. Understanding that the higher power's plan includes your growth and protection helps to reframe fear as an opportunity for development rather than a threat.

Embracing a mindset of gratitude can also diminish fear. By focusing on the positive aspects of your life and the blessings you have, you shift your attention from what you fear to what you are grateful for. This shift in focus can reduce anxiety and help you approach fear with a more balanced perspective.

Ultimately, overcoming fear involves cultivating trust in the higher power's plan and protection. By embracing the divine guidance available to you, taking proactive steps, and seeking support, you can transform fear into a catalyst for growth and empowerment.

The Meaning of Life: Discovering Your Purpose

The quest for meaning is a fundamental aspect of the human experience. We often search for purpose and direction, seeking answers to the profound question: Why am I here? The belief in a higher power provides a transformative perspective on this quest, revealing that our lives are part of a grand, divine plan imbued with purpose and significance.

Understanding that there is a higher power guiding and shaping our existence can profoundly impact our search for meaning. This belief suggests that our lives are not random or accidental but are part of a purposeful design. Each moment, each experience, is woven into a larger narrative that contributes to our individual and collective growth.

The journey to discovering your purpose begins with recognizing that you are an integral part of the higher power's plan. Every person is created with unique gifts, talents, and potential, contributing to the divine design in ways that are often beyond our immediate understanding. Embracing this notion helps shift the focus from self-doubt and uncertainty to a sense of belonging and importance within a greater scheme.

Exploring your purpose involves reflecting on your passions, talents, and values. These elements often provide clues about where you fit into the higher power's plan. What activities bring you joy? What causes resonate deeply with you? What skills do you possess that you feel compelled to share? These reflections can guide you toward understanding how your unique attributes contribute to a larger purpose.

Trusting that the higher power's plan includes your well-being and growth helps to align your efforts with a sense of greater meaning. Even when faced with challenges or setbacks, believe that these experiences are part of the divine plan, shaping you and preparing you for the fulfillment of your purpose. This trust can provide a sense of reassurance and motivation, knowing that every experience is contributing to your journey.

Another way to discover your purpose is through service and connection with others. Engaging in acts of kindness, contributing to your community, and building relationships can reveal aspects of your purpose. Often, purpose is found in how we impact and uplift those around us. By serving others and sharing your gifts, you align with the higher power's plan and uncover deeper layers of meaning in your life.

Personal growth and self-discovery are integral to understanding your purpose. Embrace opportunities for learning and development, as these experiences can reveal new dimensions of your purpose. The higher power's plan often includes growth through various experiences, helping you uncover and embrace your true calling.

Remember that the search for meaning is a continuous journey rather than a destination. Life's purpose is not a static concept but an evolving understanding that unfolds as you grow and experience new aspects of life. Trust that the higher power is guiding you through this process, revealing your purpose in stages as you progress.

Embracing the idea that your life is part of a higher power's plan can transform your perspective on challenges and achievements. Each step you take, each choice you make, contributes to the fulfillment of a grand design. By aligning your actions with the higher power's guidance and remaining open to the evolving nature of your purpose, you find meaning in the journey itself.

Ultimately, discovering your purpose involves recognizing that your life is a vital part of a larger divine plan. By reflecting on your passions, serving others, embracing personal growth, and trusting in the higher power's guidance, you uncover the meaning and significance of your existence. This understanding provides a profound sense of fulfillment, knowing that your life contributes to a greater, benevolent design.

Surrendering to the Higher Power's Will

The concept of letting go can be both liberating and daunting. It requires us to release our tight grip on control and embrace the notion that there is a higher power guiding our journey. Surrendering to the higher power's will is not about giving up but about finding freedom in trust and acceptance. This surrender brings a profound sense of peace and allows us to navigate life with a renewed perspective.

Letting go begins with acknowledging that certain aspects of life are beyond our control. We often strive to manage every detail, fearing that without our intervention, things will fall apart. However, recognizing that the higher power oversees the broader scope of existence allows us to release this burden. By surrendering control, we align ourselves with a greater plan, trusting that the higher power's wisdom surpasses our own.

Surrendering to the higher power's will is a journey of trust. It involves believing that there is a divine purpose behind every event and every decision, even when we cannot see it. This trust means accepting that some outcomes are not meant to be, and that what may initially seem like setbacks are often stepping stones to a larger, benevolent plan. By embracing this trust, we free ourselves from the stress and anxiety of trying to orchestrate every detail of our lives.

In letting go, we also release the fear of uncertainty. Life is inherently unpredictable, and the need for certainty can lead to anxiety and frustration. Surrendering to the higher power's will allows us to find comfort in the unknown. We accept that while we cannot foresee every twist and turn, the higher power's guidance will lead us where we need to go. This acceptance fosters a sense of freedom and opens us to the possibilities that lie beyond our limited vision.

Embracing the freedom of letting go also involves relinquishing our attachments to specific outcomes. We often cling to our own plans and desires, believing that they are the only path to happiness. However, surrendering to the higher power's will means opening ourselves to the possibility that there may be a different, even better path than we initially envisioned. By releasing our attachment to how things should be, we allow ourselves to experience life more fully and authentically.

Letting go does not mean passivity or inaction. It is an active choice to align with the higher power's will while continuing to take deliberate steps in our own lives. It involves discerning when to act and when to release control, finding the balance between personal effort and divine guidance. This dynamic interplay of action and surrender allows us to move forward with purpose while remaining open to the higher power's direction.

Practicing gratitude can enhance the experience of letting go. By focusing on what we have and the blessings that already surround us, we shift our attention from what we lack or fear. Gratitude helps us appreciate the present moment and trust that everything is unfolding as it should. This positive perspective reinforces our surrender and strengthens our connection with the higher power's plan.

Ultimately, the freedom found in letting go lies in the peace that comes from trusting in a higher power's will.

By surrendering our need for control and embracing the divine guidance available to us, we find a sense of liberation and serenity. This surrender allows us to navigate life's challenges with grace, knowing that we are supported by a force greater than ourselves.

In letting go, we discover the true essence of freedom—freedom from anxiety, freedom from the burden of control, and freedom to embrace life as it unfolds. By surrendering to the higher power's will, we align ourselves with a greater purpose and experience the profound peace that comes from trusting in the divine plan.

Higher Power's Plan for Every Stage of Life

When we reach a certain age, it's not uncommon to question our relevance or purpose, especially if we feel that our best years are behind us. This mindset can lead to a sense of despair or resignation, as if life has passed us by and there's little left to contribute. However, embracing the belief that every stage of life is part of a higher power's plan offers a transformative perspective, reminding us that our journey is far from over.

The notion that your age limits your potential is a misconception that overlooks the higher power's boundless wisdom and purpose. The divine plan is not constrained by time or age; rather, it encompasses every phase of our lives, offering opportunities for growth, contribution, and renewal. Every moment, regardless of our age, is an opportunity to align with the higher power's plan and find new purpose.

In recognizing that age is not a barrier but a stage in the unfolding divine plan, we open ourselves to new possibilities. The higher power's plan is not static; it evolves with us, adapting to our changing circumstances and providing fresh avenues for fulfillment. Whether you're transitioning into retirement, starting a new venture, or exploring new interests, there is always a place for you in the grand design.

Embracing this perspective involves letting go of societal expectations and self-imposed limitations. Society often has rigid ideas about what is appropriate at certain ages, but the higher power's plan transcends these constraints. By releasing these limiting beliefs, you allow yourself to explore new paths and embrace opportunities that may have previously seemed out of reach.

Each stage of life brings unique gifts and perspectives that can be valuable to the higher power's plan. The wisdom accumulated over the years, the experiences you've lived through, and the insights you've gained are all assets that contribute to a richer, more nuanced understanding of life. These elements are not to be discarded but embraced as vital components of your ongoing journey.

In moments of doubt or transition, reflect on how you can contribute to the world in new ways. The higher power's plan for you may involve different forms of service, learning, or creation that align with your current stage of life. By staying open to these possibilities, you can continue to find meaning and purpose, regardless of your age.

It's also important to embrace the joy of new beginnings. Age can bring a sense of liberation and freedom to pursue passions or dreams that may have been set aside earlier in life. This freedom to reinvent yourself or explore new interests is a testament to the higher power's ongoing involvement in your journey.

Remember that every phase of life is an opportunity to grow closer to the divine plan. Your age does not diminish your value or potential; it enhances it by adding depth and richness to your experience. The higher power's plan for you is always evolving, and your role within it is as significant now as it has ever been.

As you navigate this stage of life, trust in the higher power's plan and embrace the possibilities it offers. Let go of the notion that your best years are behind you and instead focus on the present moment, where new opportunities and experiences await. By aligning with the divine plan and recognizing the value of every stage of life, you find renewed purpose and fulfillment, knowing that you are always a vital part of the grand design.

Embrace the Higher Power's Plan with an Open Heart

As we journey through life, it is natural to encounter moments of uncertainty, challenge, and introspection. The essence of navigating these experiences lies in our ability to embrace the higher power's plan with an open heart and unwavering trust. This trust is the cornerstone of finding meaning, purpose, and peace amidst the ever-changing currents of our existence.

To embrace the higher power's plan is to acknowledge that there is a divine orchestration at work in every aspect of our lives. It means recognizing that, even when we cannot see the full picture, there is a greater design unfolding that is both purposeful and benevolent. This acknowledgment allows us to release our need for control and find solace in the knowledge that we are guided by a force far greater than ourselves.

Living with an open heart involves embracing the present moment with acceptance and gratitude. It means being receptive to the lessons and opportunities that come our way, even if they are not what we had anticipated. By approaching life with this openness, we align ourselves with the higher power's intentions and allow ourselves to fully experience the richness of each moment.

Trusting in the higher power's plan also requires letting go of the fear of the unknown. It involves surrendering our anxieties about what the future holds and finding comfort in the assurance that we are supported and guided. This trust is not passive; it is an active engagement with life, where we move forward with faith, knowing that every step is part of a greater journey.

In moments of distress or doubt, remind yourself of the higher power's constant presence and unwavering support. Even when answers are not immediately clear or when the path seems obscured, trust that there is a purpose and a plan that is unfolding for your ultimate good. Embrace these moments as opportunities for growth and reflection, knowing that they are integral to the divine design.

As you move forward, carry with you the knowledge that you are never alone in your journey. The higher power's plan encompasses every joy, every challenge, and every transition, weaving them into a tapestry of purpose and meaning. Embrace this plan with confidence and gratitude, knowing that you are a cherished part of a grand, unfolding story.

Ultimately, embracing the higher power's plan with an open heart and trust transforms the way we experience life. It shifts our focus from the immediate and the uncertain to the profound and the eternal. By aligning ourselves with this divine plan, we find peace in the midst of chaos, purpose in the midst of uncertainty, and joy in the midst of the ordinary.

May you carry this understanding with you, knowing that each moment is a testament to the higher power's love and guidance. Embrace the journey with faith, and let your heart be open to the endless possibilities that lie within the divine plan.

Printed in Great Britain
by Amazon

61547344R00057